Sandra Nicholls   Patrick O'Shea   Tony Yeadon

©Sandra Nicholls Patrick O'Shea Tony Yeadon 1977

First published 1977
by Edward Arnold (Publishers) Ltd
25 Hill Street
London W1X 8LL

ISBN: 0 7131 0115 6

All Rights Reserved. No part of this publication may be
reproduced, stored in a retrieval system, or transmitted
in any form or by any means, electronic, mechanical,
photocopying, recording or otherwise, without the prior
permission of Edward Arnold (Publishers) Ltd.

Setting, illustrations and design:
Parkway Group, 119 Parkway, London NW1 7PS

Printed in Great Britain
by Butler and Tanner Ltd, Frome and London.

What's your name, please?

Man	Good morning.
Woman	Good morning. What's your name, please?
Man	Brian Ford.
Woman	Mr. B. Ford—Flight 312?
Man	Yes, that's right.
Woman	Thank you Mr. Ford.

One

Man	What's your name, please?
Woman	Anne Scott.
Man	Anne Scott—Ah, yes. Room 231.
Woman	Thank you very much.
Man	Not at all.

Two

Policeman	Your name, please.
Eric Nielsen	Pardon?
Policeman	What's your name, please?
Eric Nielsen	Eric Nielsen.
Policeman	Thank you.

Three

Practice

a

Complete this.

Man   Good afternoon.
Woman   _afternoon._
             name?
Man   _David_
Woman   _Mr_ _213?_
Man   _Yes,_
Woman   _Mr Steele._

Chris   Hello. My name's Chris.
Sarah   Oh, hello. My name's Sarah.
Chris   Would you like a coffee?
Sarah   Mmm. Yes, please.

4 Four

b

Complete this.

Gordon   _Hello_ _name's Gordon_
Anne   _My_
Gordon   _Would_ _a drink?_
Anne   _Mmm._

c

Complete this.

Brian _____
_____
Eric _____
_____
Brian _____
_____
Eric _____

What's his name?

Mrs. Wilson	What's his name?
Steve Wilson	Jimmy Starr.
Mrs. Wilson	Jimmy Starr?
Steve	Yes, Mum. He's a pop singer.
Mrs. Wilson	And what's . . .
Steve	Shhh! Mum!
Mrs. Wilson	Sorry.

Five

Steve	What's her job?
Mike Wilson	She's a reporter.
Steve	A newspaper reporter?
Mike	No, a TV reporter.
Steve	Oh, what's her name?
Mike	Sarah Goodwin.

Six

Practice

Answer the questions.

What's her name? _____

And what's her job? _____

Ask the questions.

_____ Jimmy Starr.

_____ He's a pop singer.

Answer the questions.

What's your name?   My _____

What's (What is)	my your his her	name ?

My Your His Her	name's (name is)	_____ _____ _____

What's (What is)	my your his her	job?

I'm (I am) You're (You are) He's (He is) She's (She is)	a	pop singer. newspaper reporter. T.V. reporter. policeman.

Ask and answer questions.

_____ name?

_____ ?

businessman.

_____ name?

_____ ?

secretary.

Where are you from?

2

Officer	What's your name, please?
Sheila	Sheila Martin.
Officer	And where are you from?
Sheila	Sydney, Australia.
Officer	What's your job?
Sheila	I'm a secretary.
Officer	Are you here on holiday?
Sheila	Yes, I am.
Officer	Thank you, Miss Martin.

7 Seven

8 Eight

Sarah	Who's that?
Anne	Brian Ford.
Sarah	Where's he from?
Anne	He's from England.
Sarah	From Manchester?
Anne	No, London.
Sarah	What's his job?
Anne	He's a sales manager.

Practice

Ask and answer the questions.

a

What's his name? — His name is Gordon Patel

What's his job? — He's a doctor

Where's he from? — He's from India

b

What's his name? — His

What's — He's

Where's

c

What's her

d

e

f

What's your name?

What's your job?

Where are you from?

Are you English? No, I'm not

Sheila	Ow!
Chris	I'm very sorry.
Sheila	Oh, that's all right.
Chris	Are you English?
Sheila	No, I'm not. I'm Australian.
Chris	Would you like a drink?
Sheila	Thanks. A lager, please.

Gordon	Is she from Australia?
Chris	Yes, she is.
Gordon	Mmm. She's pretty.

Chris	Here you are.
Sheila	What is it?
Chris	It's Carlsberg.
Sheila	Carlsberg?
Chris	Yes, it's Danish . . . it's nice.
Sheila	Thanks. Cheers!
Chris	Cheers!

Practice

Ask and answer the questions.   What day is it today?   It's _____

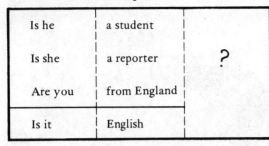

| Is he | a student |
| Is she | a reporter | ?
| Are you | from England |
| Is it | English |

Yes,	he is.
	she is.
	I am.
	it is.

No,	he isn't.
	she isn't.
	I'm not.
	it isn't.

a   Is he a policeman? No, he _____
    Is he a pop singer? Yes, _____

b   Is she from Japan? _____
    _____ Australia?
    _____

c   Are you from England
    Are you from _____?
    Yes, _____

d   Is it English? _____
    _____ Danish

Complete this.

Brian Ford: Here
Eric Neilsen: Thank you. What _____?
Brian Ford: It's Guinness
Eric Neilsen: _____
Brian Ford: Yes it's Irish
           It's _____
Eric Neilsen: _____
Brian Ford: _____

Complete these.

Example: He's from England. He's English.
_____ She's Australian.
_____ He's Danish.
_____ She's Japanese.

_____ She's French
_____ He's Spanish
_____ She's Greek
_____ He's Iranian

Is this your bus?

3

Mike	Hello, Jim. How are you?
Bus driver	Fine thanks. And you?
Mike	Not bad, thanks. Is this your bus, Jim?
Driver	No, that's my bus over there.
Mike	Oh, good. Cup of tea?
Driver	Yes, why not?

12 Twelve

Driver	Is that your mother, Mike?
Mike	Where? There? No, this is my mother.
Driver	Where?
Mike	Here, behind you. Mum, this is Jim.
Driver	Hello, Mrs. Wilson.

13 Thirteen

Mrs. Wilson	Hello, Jim.
Mike	Cup of tea, Mum?
Mrs. Wilson	Lovely!

14 Fourteen

9

Practice

Ask and answer questions.

What day is it today? _____

a. You → You write: Is this your car?

b. He → You write: Is that his car?

c. He → _____

d. You → _____

e. Me → _____

f. She/No → _____ No, it isn't.

g. Me/Yes → _____

h. You/No → _____

i. He/No → _____

j. She/Yes → _____

Gordon: Hello, _____ How _____?
Chris: Fine _____ And _____?
Gordon: Not _____
_____ car?
Chris: No, _____
_____
Gordon: Oh, _____
_____ coffee?
Chris: _____

What colour is it?

Kevin Wilson	What's that?
Pat Wilson	It's a banana.
Kevin	What colour is it?
Pat	It's yellow, dear.

Kevin	What's that?
Pat	It's a tomato.
Kevin	What colour is it?
Pat	It's red, dear.

Kevin	And that, Mum?
Pat	A lettuce.
Kevin	And what colour is it?
Pat	It's green.

Kevin	And that, Mum?
Pat	A carrot.
Kevin	What colour is . . .?
Pat	It's orange, dear, orange.

Kevin	What's that?
Pat	It's a potato.
Kevin	Wh . . .?
Pat	It's brown, dear, brown.

Kevin	Wh . . . What's that, Mum?
Pat	A bird, a bird! It's a bird.
Kevin	Wh . . .?
Pat	Blue. It's blue, blue! It's a BIRD AND IT'S BLUE!

5 Fifteen

Practice

Ask and answer questions.

Gordon Patel   My flag's green, white and orange.

Brian Ford. My flag's white and ___

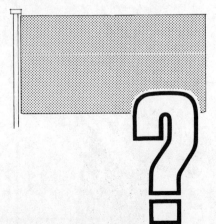

What colour's your flag?
My ___

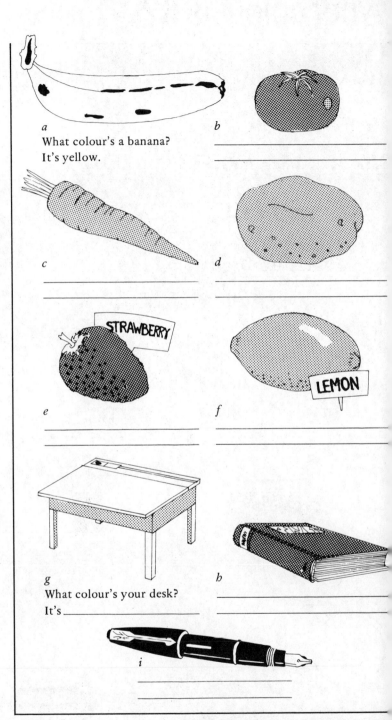

a What colour's a banana?
   It's yellow.

b ___

c ___

d ___

e ___

f ___

g What colour's your desk?
   It's ___

h ___

i ___

What day is it today?

	Monday.
It's	Tuesday.
	Wednesday.
	Thursday.
	Friday.
Today's	Saturday.
	Sunday.

This is a nice house

Assistant	Err, this is a nice house, madam.
Sarah Goodwin	Yes, but it isn't very big.

16 Sixteen

7 Seventeen

Assistant	Ah, well, here's a big house.
Sarah	Yes, but it's not very attractive.

8 Eighteen

Assistant	Well, *this* is an attractive house, madam.
Sarah	Yes, but not very modern.

9 Nineteen

Assistant	O.K. Here's a modern house.
Sarah	But it's expensive.

21 Twenty one

0 Twenty

Assistant	All right! This is a cheap house.
Sarah	Mmm. Cheap but small.

Sarah	Ah, that's an interesting house.
Assistant	Yes, but it's my house, Madam, and it's not for sale.

13

Practice

Ask and answer questions.

a What's this?
It's a banana.

b What's this?
It's an

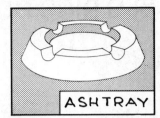
c What's this?
It's an _____

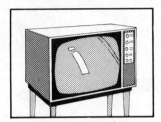
d What's this?
_____

e _____

f _____

g _____

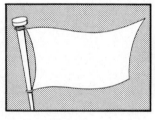
h _____

i _____

j What's this?
It's a small house.

k What's that?
It's a small house.

l _____

m _____

n _____

o _____

How much is that suit?

Assistant	Good morning, sir. Can I help you?
Chris	Yes—how much is that suit?
Assistant	The brown suit, sir?
Chris	Yes, that's right.
Assistant	Err—just a minute, sir. It's ninety pounds.
Chris	Oh dear, that's very expensive.
Assistant	But it's very good quality, sir.

Anne	Excuse me.
Assistant	Yes?
Anne	How much is this dress?
Assistant	The price is on this ticket, Madam.
Anne	Oh, yes. Eleven pounds, fifty. What size is it?
Assistant	Size twelve.
Anne	Oh, good. That's just right.

Practice

Ask and answer questions.

a How much is the suit?
  It's £55.

b _____?
  _____

c _____?
  _____

d _____?
  _____
  _____

e _____?
  _____
  _____

f _____?
  _____
  _____

g _____?
  _____

h _____?
  _____

i _____?
  _____

Complete these.

j Excuse me?
  Yes?
  _____
  _____

k How much is that coat?
  price   ticket
  Oh. Yes   pounds

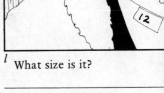

l What size is it?
  _____
  good. That's

m _____
  _____
  _____

_____
_____
_____

o _____
  _____
  _____

No, we're secretaries

Chris	Hello. I'm Chris and this is Gordon.
Sheila	Hello.
Gordon	Would you like a cigarette?
Sheila	No, thank you.
Chris	Would you like a drink?
Anne	No, thanks.

Chris	Are you nurses?
Sheila	No, we're secretaries.
Gordon	Are you secretaries in this hospital?
Anne	No, but our friends are.
Gordon	Are they here?
Anne	Yes, they're behind you.

Chris	Hello. I'm Chris and this is Gordon.
Girls	Hello.
Chris	Would you like a drink?
Girls	Yes please.
Gordon	What would you like?
Girl 1	A glass of wine, please.
Girl 2	. . . and a Coke, please.

Practice

We		assistants.
You	're	drivers.
They		Australian.

We		reporters.
You	aren't	children.
They		German.

Make these into sentences.

please/name/your/what's
What's your name, please?

Coffee/like/you/a/would?

from/Where/and/you/are?

Italian/no/not/I'm

England/you/from/Are?

like/you/What/would?

how/Mrs Wilson/Hello/you/are?

Now/is/madam/this/house/nice/a

Yes/you/behind/they're

boyfriends/aren't/Our/students.

	we	doctors?
Are	you	students?
	they	English?

Yes	we	are.
	you	
No	they	aren't.

Question   Would you like a cup of coffee?

Answer   Yes, please.
         or No, thanks.

a

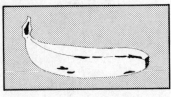

b _____

c _____

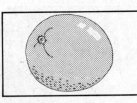

d _____

e _____

f _____

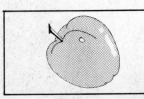

g _____

How much are those apples?

Sarah Goodwin	How much are those apples?
Assistant	These apples, madam, are ...er... just a moment.

Assistant	George. How much are these apples?
George	Which apples?
Assistant	These.
George	Ah! Those are 6p each.

Sarah	6p each for these?
Assistant	Well, they're very nice.

Sarah	How much are those?
Assistant	They're 4p each.
Sarah	Fine. One please.

Practice

Complete these

a

How much are these apples?
These are

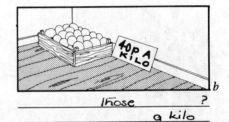
b

Those ?
a kilo

c

These ?

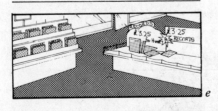
d

f

Complete these.

This coat is cheap → These coats are cheap.

That house is small ___
This woman is old ___
That student is young ___
This apple is nice ___

That nurse is attractive ___
This book is expensive ___
That bird is blue ___
That man's from England ___

Revision

Fill in the blanks.

a)
Name: JIMMY STARR
Job: POP SINGER
Country: ENGLAND

_____ name? _____ Starr.
_____ job? _____
_____ from? _____

b)
Name: GORDON PATEL
Job: DOCTOR
Country: INDIA

c)
Name: MIKE WILSON
Job: BUS DRIVER
Country: ENGLAND

d)
Name: SHEILA MARTIN
Job: SECRETARY
Country: AUSTRALIA

	You write:	
e) reporter?	Is she a reporter?	Yes, she is.
Australia?	Is she Australian?	No, she isn't.
f) policeman?		
England		
g) businessman?		
Greece?		
h) student?		
Australia?		
i) pop-singer?		
England?		
j) bus-driver?		
Denmark?		

Make these into sentences.

Chris/Hello. are/How/you?
thanks/fine/I'm. you/And?
thank/well/Very/you.
coffee/like/a/of/cup/you/Would?
you/thank/No.

Ask and answer questions.

a
Is this your car?
Yes, it is.

b
that
Yes

c
No

d
No

e
Yes

f
No

g
No

h
No

Ask and answer questions.

a) What colour's a tomato?   It's red.
b) carrot?
c) lemon?
d) banana?
e) lettuce?
f) orange?

This is Jim Smith. He's a bus driver and he's from London. This is his car. It's a red Ford. It's modern but not very expensive. And that's his wife. Her name's Brenda. She's from Manchester and she's a nurse. Her bicycle is beside her. It's old and it isn't very nice, but it's cheap.

Ask and answer.

a) name? _What's his name?_ _Jim Smith / His name's Jim Smith._
b) job? _____
c) from? _____
d) car/a Ford? _____
e) modern? _____
f) very expensive? _____
g) that/wife? _____
h) name? _____
i) job? _____
j) where/her bicycle? _____
k) new? _____
l) cheap? _____

Complete this:

Angus Stuart/taxi driver/Edinburgh. Car/black and white/Volvo/modern/very expensive/Wife/Mary/Glasgow/hairdresser. Car/new/very nice/but it isn't cheap.

Now ask questions about Angus Stuart.

a) taxi driver? _____
b) Edinburgh? _____
c) Car/Mercedes? _____
d) colour/taxi? _____

Now answer the questions.

23

Complete these.

a _____ these _____ ?

b _____ those _____ ?

c _____

d _____

e _____

f _____

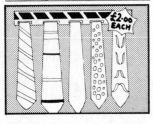
g _____

h _____

i _____

Complete this crossword.

CLUES

Across
3. Jimmy Starr is a _ _ _ _ _ _ _ _ _ (9)
8. Red and blue _ _ _ colours. (3)
9. She's from Australia _ _ _ name's Sheila. (3)
11. Would you like a drink? No, _ _ _ _ _ _ _ _ _ (5,3)
14. No, Sheila _ _ _ _ from London. (4)
15. How _ _ _ _ _ is that coat? (5)

CLUES

Down
1. Gordon is a _ _ _ _ _ _ (6)
2. A tomato _ _ red. (2)
4. My _ _ _ _ is Peter. (4)
5 & 7. Those apples are 5p _ _ _ _ (4)
6. Jimmy Starr: "This is my _ _ _ (3) and these are my friends."
10. Those oranges are 50p a _ _ _ _ (4)
12. Are you a policeman? No, I'm _ _ _ (3)
13. Are you here _ _ holiday? (2)

I'm painting a picture of my house

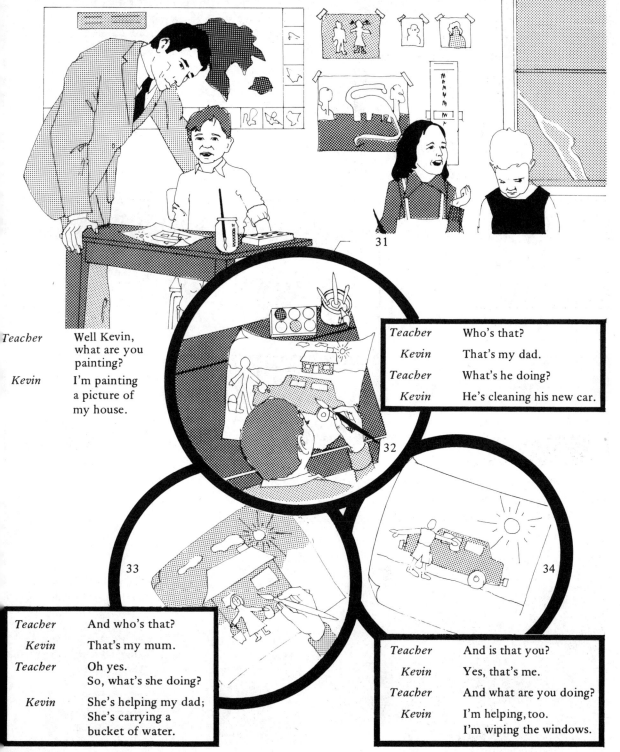

Teacher	Well Kevin, what are you painting?
Kevin	I'm painting a picture of my house.

Teacher	Who's that?
Kevin	That's my dad.
Teacher	What's he doing?
Kevin	He's cleaning his new car.

Teacher	And who's that?
Kevin	That's my mum.
Teacher	Oh yes. So, what's she doing?
Kevin	She's helping my dad; She's carrying a bucket of water.

Teacher	And is that you?
Kevin	Yes, that's me.
Teacher	And what are you doing?
Kevin	I'm helping, too. I'm wiping the windows.

Practice

What	am	I	painting
	are	you	doing
	is	he	cleaning
		she	cooking

I	am	painting a picture.
You	are	reading.
He	is	cleaning his car.
She	is	cooking a meal.

Make questions and answers for these pictures.

Example:

a

You write: What's Brian Ford doing? He's cleaning his car.

b

c

d

e

f

g

Look at this picture and then answer the questions.

1. Where are these people?
2. Where's Mr Brown sitting?
3. What's he reading?
4. What's he smoking?
5. What's Mrs Brown doing?
6. What's the little girl's name?
7. Where is she?
8. What's she doing?
9. Where's Tim sitting?
10. What's he doing?
11. Where's Jane?
12. What's she doing?

He's getting out of his car

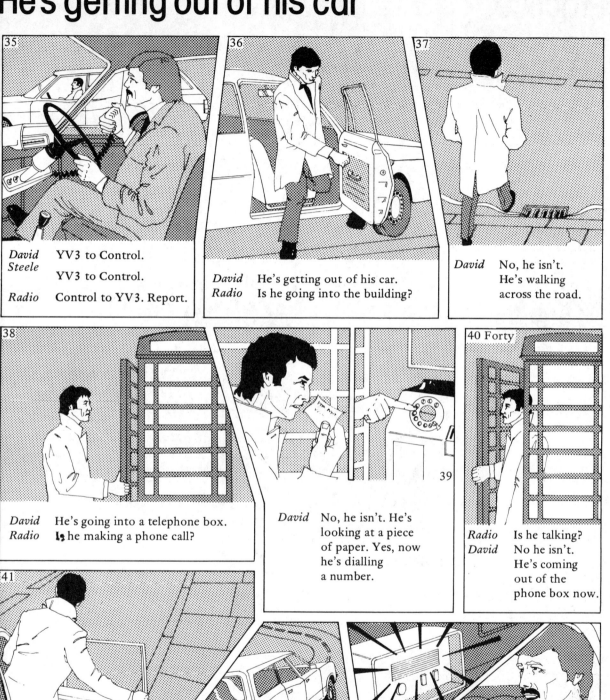

David Steele	YV3 to Control.
	YV3 to Control.
Radio	Control to YV3. Report.

David	He's getting out of his car.
Radio	Is he going into the building?

David	No, he isn't. He's walking across the road.

David	He's going into a telephone box.
Radio	Is he making a phone call?

David	No, he isn't. He's looking at a piece of paper. Yes, now he's dialling a number.

Radio	Is he talking?
David	No he isn't. He's coming out of the phone box now.

David	He's getting into his car.

David	Now he's driving down the street.

Radio	Which street?
David	Dover street.
Radio	Follow him!
David	OK. YV3 out.

Practice

Am	I	talking?	Yes, I am./No, I'm not.	I'm not talking.
Are	you	painting?	Yes, you are./No, you aren't.	You aren't painting.
Is	he	talking?	Yes, he is./No, he isn't.	He isn't talking.
	she	eating?	Yes, she is./No, she isn't.	She isn't eating.
	it	raining?	Yes, it is./No, it isn't.	It isn't raining.

You write:

Is he cleaning his car?
No, he isn't. He's reading a book.

a

_____ working?
No, _____

b

_____ television?
_____

c

_____ home today?
_____

d

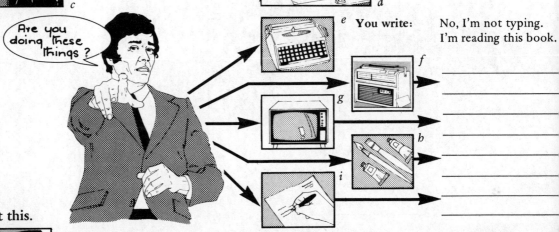

e You write: No, I'm not typing. I'm reading this book.

f _____
g _____
h _____
i _____
_____

Look at this.

going/telephone box David He's going into a telephone box.
Which?   Radio Which telephone box?
in Dover Street   David The telephone box in Dover Street.

Complete these.

coming/cinema _____
Which?   _____
in Gale Road   _____

going/police station _____
Which?   _____
in Saxby Avenue   _____

playing/park   _____
Which?   _____
in Kinson Road _____

going/greengrocer's _____
Which?   _____
in Vine Road   _____

They're having a party

Brian	What time is it, Cathy?
Cathy	Er... It's 2 o'clock.
Brian	What are they doing upstairs?
Cathy	They're having a party.
Brian	A party! At 2 o'clock!

Brian	What time is it now?
Cathy	3 o'clock.
Cathy	Where are you going?
Brian	Upstairs. They're making a terrible noise.

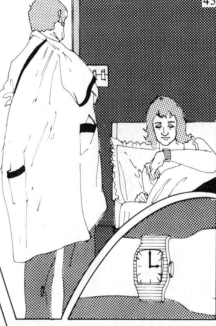

Brian	Excuse me. I'm from flat 32 downstairs............
Man	Come in. We're having a party...
Brian	...... And you're making an awful noise. It's 3 o'clock.

Man	Oh, dear. Well, come in and have a drink.
Brian	Er..No... Well, OK, thank you.

Practice

It's one o'clock. What are David Steele and the policeman doing? They're talking to Steve Wilson.

_____ they _____?

_____ ?

Teacher: _____ ?   Teacher: _____ house, too
Children: _____ house.   Children: _____ garage

What _____
What are you doing? _____

Look at these pictures carefully and say what these people are doing.
Turn the page round to find the answers!

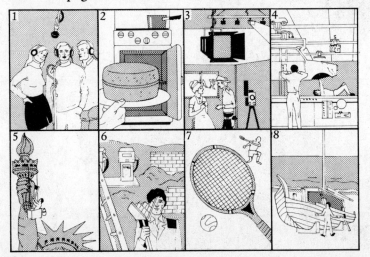

They're making a record.
He's making a cake.
They're making a film.
They're making cars.
They're cleaning the Statue of Liberty.
They're building a garage.
They're playing tennis.
They're building a boat.

These are our suitcases

Cathy — Those two people are taking our suitcases.
Brian — You're right, so they are.

Brian — Excuse me. What are you doing with our suitcases?
Man — Your suitcases! These are our suitcases..... look at the label.

Brian — Hmmm . . . yes. Yes they are. Sorry!
Man — That's all right.

Brian — Oh, yes. I'm sorry. Well where are our suitcases, then?
Woman — Are those your suitcases, over there?

Woman — Their suitcases!! Huh!
Man — Well, they *are* the same colour.

Practice

	my	car.
It's	your	book.
	his	table.
	her	cigarette.
	our	suitcases.
They're	your	tickets.
	their	sandwiches.

Cathy Those two people are taking our suitcases.
Brian You're right. So they are.

Now write sentences for these other pictures.

_____

   A Excuse me! Are these your suitcases?
B Yes, they are.
A Oh! I'm sorry.

   A _____
B _____
A _____

   A _____
B _____
A _____

   A _____
B _____
A _____

   *Examples*:   You write   It's his watch

32

It's mine!

9

David Steele	Whose watch is this?
Steve Wilson	It's my watch.
David	No, it isn't. It's Mrs Ford's watch.
Steve	No, it isn't! It's mine!
Cathy Ford	Nonsense! It's mine.

David	Is this your lighter?
Cathy	Yes, it is.
Steve	Your lighter?—That's mine.
David	No, Steve. It's hers, isn't it?

David	Now Steve, whose clock is this?
Steve	It's my brother's. Really. It's his.
David	No, it isn't. It's hers.

David	Now, Mrs Wilson, whose rings are these? Are they really yours?
Mrs Wilson	No, Mr. Steele, they aren't mine.
Steve	Yes, they are Mum. They're yours.
Mrs Wilson	No, Steve, they aren't mine.
Steve	Oh, Mum!!

Practice

Look at these questions and answers.

Whose paintings are these? → They're Mrs Ford's paintings.
→ They're Mrs Ford's.

Whose lighter is this? → It's Mrs Ford's lighter.
→ It's Mrs Ford's.

Now, ask and answer questions.

a Whose shirt is this?

b

c

d

e

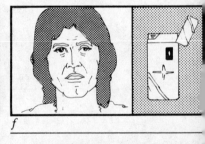

f

g Whose house is this?
It's his.

h

i

j Are these Sarah Goodwin's?
No, they aren't Sarah's.
They're hers.

k Cathy Ford's?

l Mike Wilson's

34

They aren't ours, are they?

Sheila   Look, Chris. Whose tickets are those?
Chris   They aren't ours, are they?
Sheila   No, ours are in my handbag.

Chris   Excuse me! Are these yours?
Man   No, they aren't ours.

Chris   They aren't theirs, Sheila.
Sheila   Oh look! Ask those people in front.

Chris   Excuse me! Are these your tickets?
Girl   No, they're not ours.

Chris   Excuse me. Are these yours?
Woman   Our tickets! Thank goodness! Thanks very much.
Chris   That's all right.

Practice

It's my car.　　　　It's your dress.　　　It's his watch.　　　They're her rings.
It's mine.　　　　　It's yours.　　　　　It's his.　　　　　　They're hers.

They're our records.　It's your house.　　They're their tickets.
They're ours.　　　　It's yours.　　　　　They're theirs.

Fill in the blanks.

A Hey! That _____'s _____
B No, _____ it's _____
A It's _____ It's _____ new car.
B _____ not four _____, it's

B Is that _____, behind
   red
A Oh! Yes, I'm _____ They're
   same colour.

Ask and answer questions.

a Prompt: your/no
   Question That's your car,
             isn't it?
   Answer No, it isn't mine.

b their/yes

c his/no

d her/yes

e your/no

f his/yes

g her/no

h your/yes

I've got a large office

10

Anne	I've got a new boss.
Sarah	Oh, what's he like?
Anne	Well, he's got dark hair and brown eyes . . .
Sarah	Yes . . .
Anne	And a white sports car . . .
Sarah	Hmmm . . . that's good.
Anne	Yes, but he's got a wife and three children as well!

62

David Steele	What's your new job like?
Brian Ford	Oh, it's fine. I've got a very nice secretary and a large pleasant office...
David	Hm.
Brian	And a company car.
David	Very nice.
Brian	Yes, it is . . . but I've got a lot of work, too!
David	Well, that's life, isn't it?

63

Practice

I've You've We've They've	got	a large office. a very pleasant secretary. a company car. dark hair.
He's She's		brown eyes. a sports car.

This is a special announcement.
The police are looking for a dangerous criminal. His name is Gerry Smith and he is twenty five years old.
He's got short dark hair and grey eyes. He is about six feet tall and he's got a scar on his chin . . . . . .

Write the same kind of 'special' announcement' about these criminals.

	Bill Daly	**George Cutler**	**Joe Watts**	**Larry Moon**
Hair	Long dark	short fair	long straight	short curly
Eyes	brown	blue	green	grey
Scar	chin	cheek	nose	forehead
Height	5' 6" 1m 68	6' 3" 1m 90	5' 11" 1m 80	4' 10" 1m 47
Age	44	28	36	57

Now describe
(a) yourself (b) the person sitting next to you.

What have you got in that bag?

Steve	Is that you George?
George	Yeah.
Steve	Well, I've got the tools.
George	Fine. What've you got?
Steve	I've got a hammer, a pair of gloves, a file and some keys.
George	What about screwdrivers?
Steve	Yes, I've got some screwdrivers.
George	Fine. See you later then.
Steve	O.K. Bye.

David Steele	What are you doing here, Wilson?
Steve	I'm waiting for a friend.
David	What have you got in that bag?
Steve	My football boots.
David	That isn't true, is it, Steve?
Steve	Yes, it is.
David	Open the bag please, constable.
Constable	Yes, sir.

David	What's he got in there?
Constable	He's got a hammer, a file, some screwdrivers and a pair of gloves.
David	What about his football boots?
Constable	No football boots, sir.
David	And what's he got in his pocket?
Constable	Er . . . some keys, sir.
David	Right, Wilson, come with me, please.

Practice

Steve Is _____ George?
George _____
Steve Well _____ fruit.
George _____ What _____?
Steve I ____ a _____, two _____,
       a _____, and same _____
George What about _____?
Steve Yes, _____
George _____ see _____
Steve _____

Cathy _____
Brian _____
Cathy _____
Brian _____
Cathy _____

Brian _____
Cathy _____
Brian _____
Cathy _____

| What've | you / they | got | in that bag? |
| What's | he / she | | |

| I've / We've / They've | got | a hammer. a pair of gloves. a file. |
| He's / She's | | some keys. some screwdrivers. |

Ask and answer the questions.

c What's Cathy Ford got in her basket?
_____
_____

d _____ Brian Ford _____?
_____
_____

haven't got a cough

Chris	Now, Mr. Wilson, what's the matter with you?
Mike	I've got a bad cold, doctor.
Chris	Have you got a cough?
Mike	No, I haven't got a cough ... but I've got a sore throat.

Chris	I see. Open your mouth, please. Say ahhh.
Mike	Ahhhhhhhh.
Chris	Hm. Have you got a pain in your chest?
Mike	No, I haven't.

Chris	Well, here's a prescription.
Mike	Thank you, doctor.
Chris	Take two pills every morning.
Mike	Yes.
Chris	And two every night. Goodbye, Mr Wilson.
Mike	Goodbye.

Chris	Oh ... Mr Wilson.
Mike	Yes?
Chris	Come and see me again next week, please.
Mike	O.K. Goodbye, doctor.
Chris	Goodbye.

Practice

Have	I you we they	got	a cold? a cough? a sore throat?
Has	he she		a pain? a head-ache?

Yes,	I you we they	have.
	he she	has.

No,	I you we they	haven't.
	he she	hasn't.

cough?

Has he got a cough?
No, he hasn't.
He's got a headache.

headache?

_____ ?
_____
_____

sore throat?

_____ ?
_____
_____

pain/leg

_____ ?
_____
_____

pain/chest?

_____ ?
_____
_____

Pain/foot?

_____ ?
_____
_____

 ← Look at these. →

He's got two pills   He hasn't got *any* pills

```
        Sally & David                         John & Julie
Clare                  Mary & Larry    Susan      Fred    George    Ann & Peter
                      Barry   Roger                                      Celia
```

Now fill in the blanks.

Sally & David
_____
_____
They haven't got any sons.
_____
_____

John & Julia
children   They have got five children.
daughters   _____
sons   _____
grandchildren   _____
grandsons   _____
grand-daughters   _____

Have you got any milk left?

Shopkeeper	Good morning, Mrs Hartley.
Mrs Hartley	Good morning. Have you got any milk left?
Shopkeeper	Just a minute. Yes, we have.
Mrs Hartley	Oh, good. I'd like two bottles, please.
Shopkeeper	Here you are.
Mrs Hartley	Thank you.

71

Shopkeeper	Anything else?
Mrs Hartley	Yes. I'd like a packet of tea and a jar of honey.
Shopkeeper	Yes.
Mrs Hartley	And have you got any Cheddar cheese?
Shopkeeper	No, I'm afraid we haven't. We've only got Cheshire cheese today.

72

Mrs Hartley	All right, a small piece of Cheshire, please.
Shopkeeper	Is this piece all right?
Mrs Hartley	Yes, that's fine.
Shopkeeper	Anything else, Mrs Hartley?
Mrs Hartley	No, thank you. How much is all that?
Shopkeeper	One pound fifteen, please.

73

Practice

 some milk / a bottle of milk   *a*

 some wine / a bottle of wine   *b*

 some tea / a packet of tea   *c*

 some sugar / a packet of sugar   *d*

 some honey / a jar of honey   *e*

 some coffee / a jar of coffee   *f*

 some cheese / a piece of cheese   *g*

 some cake / a piece of cake   *h*

Look at this dialogue.

Customer	Have you got any milk left?
Shop assistant	Just a minute, please. Yes, we have.
Customer	Oh, good. I'd like a bottle please.
Shop assistant	Here you are. Anything else?
Customer	Yes, have you got any bread?
Shop assistant	No, I'm afraid we haven't.

Now ask about these things.

a sugar/tea _____
b coffee/honey _____
c cheese/milk _____
d Chocolate cake/flour _____
e butter/rice _____
f strawberry jam/tomato sauce _____
g White wine/Coca Cola _____

Fill in the blanks.

 *i* Has he got a bottle of milk?
_____

 *j* Has he got a piece of cheese?
_____

 *k*
_____

 *l*
_____

 *m* Have you got a car?
_____

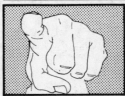 *n* Have you got any brothers?
_____

Revision

a
Whose handbag is this?

It's Anne Scott's.

b

c

d

e

f

 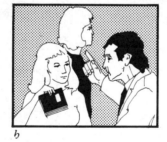 

g
Is this your pen?

No, it isn't. It's his.

h

i

j
this your bag?

es, it is. It's mine.

k

l

45

Complete the conversation.

Teacher	_____
Child	I'm drawing.
Teacher	_____
Child	A car.
Teacher	_____
Child	No, it isn't. It's my friend's car.
Teacher	_____
Child	Peter.
Teacher	_____
Child	It's red.
Teacher	_____
Child	Yes.

Ask and answer questions.

a

b

What's the time? _____

What's he doing? _____

c

It's two o'clock.

She's looking at her watch.

d

e

f

g

Fill in the blanks.

74

What's she got in her fridge? _She's got_ _____ milk
_____ packet of butter _____ wine, _____ lettuce,
_____ piece of cheese, and _____ eggs. _____
She hasn't got _____ meat.

75

What's he got in his bag? _____
He's got some _____, a _____,
a _____, some _____, a _____
_____, and a _____, He hasn't got
a _____ or any _____

Describe these people.

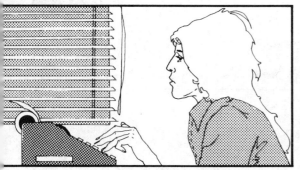

76

Sheila Martin is Australian.
She's got fair hair and blue eyes.
She's about twenty-four and she's a secretary.
At the moment she is typing a letter for her boss.

77

_____
_____
_____
_____

78

_____
_____
_____
_____

79

_____
_____
_____
_____

47

80 Eighty

Answer these questions.

1 What is Mike Wilson doing?
2 What is Pat Wilson doing?
3 Are the children reading?
4 Are the children playing with the dog?
5 Are the children playing with a ball?
6 Is Mike wearing a hat?
7 What is he smoking?
8 What is Pat wearing?
9 Is she eating a piece of cake?
10 Is the car old or new?
11 What has Pat got in her hand?
12 Is she cutting some cheese?
13 Have they got a dog?
14 Is it a small dog or a large dog?
15 What is the dog doing?

Make questions for these answers.

He's wearing a shirt and a pair of trousers.
She's cutting a cake.
No, he isn't. He's smoking a pipe.
No, they aren't. They're playing with a ball.
No, they haven't. They've got an old one.

13 There's an envelope under that file

Cathy	What are you doing, Brian?
Brian	I'm looking for some paper.
Cathy	Writing paper?
Brian	Yes.
Cathy	Well, there's some writing paper on the desk.
Brian	Oh, thanks.

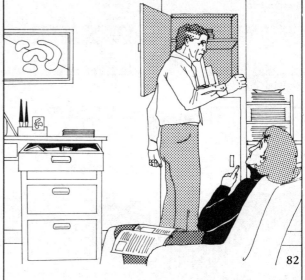

Cathy	What are you looking for now?
Brian	An envelope.
Cathy	I think there's an envelope under that file.
Brian	Oh, yes. Here it is.

Cathy	Brian?
Brian	Yes?
Cathy	Are you looking for a stamp?
Brian	Er . . . yes.
Cathy	Well, there are some in my handbag.
Brian	Oh, good. Thanks.

Brian	Cathy?
Cathy	Um?
Brian	Where is your handbag?
Cathy	Oh really, Brian. You're hopeless!

49

Practice

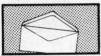
an envelope

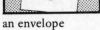
a pen

some paper

some ink

some stamps

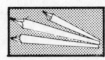
some pencils

There is	a pen an envelope some paper some ink	under that file. on the desk.
There are	some stamps some pencils	in my handbag.

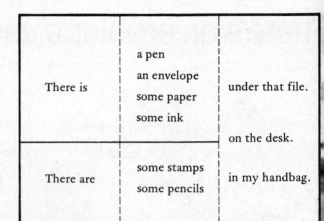

Put *a* or *some* in the blanks.

This is .... picture of Mike Wilson's living room. In the room there is .... table, ... chairs, and .... pictures. Mike is watching television. On the television there are .... flowers in .... vase. His wife is writing .... letter. On the table there is .... paper and .... ink. She's got .... stamps in her handbag. Mike and Pat have got two children, ... boy, and .... girl. The little girl is playing with .... cat under the table and the little boy is playing with .... toy cars. On the table there are .... pencils, ... newspaper and .... fruit.

Ask and answer questions about the picture.

cat/table   Is there a cat under the table?
             Yes there is.

pens/floor   _____

wine/desk   _____

pictures/table   Are there any pictures on the table?
                No, there aren't.

car/chair   _____

flowers/TV   _____

How much would you like?

Butcher	Who's next, please?
Mrs Wilson	I am. I'd like two pounds of . . .
Mrs Jones	Excuse me. You're not next. I am.
Mrs Wilson	Sorry, but I'm next.

Butcher	Come on, ladies. Make up your minds.
Mrs Wilson	I'm next and I'd like some minced meat.
Butcher	How much would you like?
Mrs Wilson	Two pounds, please.

Butcher	Anything else?
Mrs Wilson	Yes, some lamb chops.
Butcher	How many?
Mrs Wilson	Er . . . four large ones.

Butcher	Is that all?
Mrs Wilson	No. Have you got any kidneys?
Butcher	Yes, but I've only got three left.
Mrs Wilson	Those are fine.

90 Ninety

Butcher	Now, madam, what would you like?
Mrs Jones	Three kidneys, please.
Butcher	I'm sorry, madam. I haven't got any left.
Mrs Jones	Huh!

Practice

Ask and answer questions about Mrs Wilson's shopping.

Prompt sugar   How much sugar has she got?

She's got a kilo.

chops

vinegar

oranges

eggs

wine

kidneys

minced meat

How many	eggs chops apples	
		would you like?
How much	wine milk coffee	

Fill in the blanks.

Assistant	Good morning. Can I help you?	afternoon
Mrs Wilson	Yes, please. I'd like some eggs.	wine.
Assistant	How many would you like?	
Mrs Wilson	Six, please.	litres

Now make up other conversations about Mrs Wilson's shopping.

Answer these questions.

How many brothers have you got?
How many students are there in your class?
How many children have you got?
How much money have you got in your pocket/handbag?
How many sisters have you got?

I always stay at the International Hotel

Sarah Goodwin	Excuse me. I'm making a television programme about foreign visitors to Britain. Can I ask you some questions?
American	Certainly.
Sarah	Is this your first visit to Britain?
American	No, it isn't. I come to Britain every year.
Sarah	And where do you stay?
American	I always stay at the International Hotel.
Sarah	And....
American	Excuse me. My taxi is here.

Sarah	Excuse me. Where do you come from?
Japanese man	We come from Japan.
Sarah	From Tokyo?
Japanese woman	No, we live in Yokohama.
Sarah	Is this your first visit to London?
Japanese man	No, it isn't. It's our third visit.
Japanese woman	We like your country very much.
Sarah	Thank you.

Sarah	Excuse me. Where do you come from?
Man	Why? Who are you?
Sarah	I'm a television reporter and I'm making a programme about foreign visitors to Britain....
Man	Well, I'm a business man and I'm in a hurry.
Sarah	Oh, I'm sorry.
Man	And I never answer questions. Goodbye.

Practice

Interview these people.

 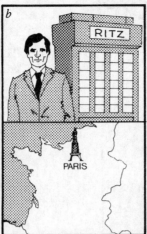 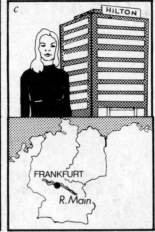 

Where do you come from?
   I come from America.
Where do you live?
   I live in New York.
Where do you stay?
   I always stay at the International Hotel.

Now answer these questions about yourself.

What's your name?............................
How old are you?...............................
Where do you come from?...................

Where do you live?.............................
What's your job?................................
Where do you work?...........................

Ask someone else these questions and fill in the form below.

Name:...............	Town/City:........................
Age:.................	Job:...............................
Country:............	Place of work:.....................

Mike and Pat Wilson are on holiday in Southend.

This is a postcard from them to Mrs Wilson.

Imagine you are on holiday. Write some postcards to your friends.

How long does the journey take?

Ticket clerk	Next, please.
Anne Scott	A ticket to Manchester, please.
Clerk	Single or return?
Anne	Return, please.
Clerk	That's seventeen pounds, forty pence.
Anne	Oh, can I pay by cheque?
Clerk	Have you got a banker's card?
Anne	Yes, I have.
Clerk	That's fine.

Anne	Oh, excuse me.
Clerk	Yes?
Anne	What's the date today?
Clerk	It's ... er ..... the fourteenth, June the fourteenth.
Clerk	Thanks.

Clerk	Fine, here is your ticket, madam.
Anne	Thank you. How long does this ticket last?
Clerk	Three months.
Anne	So, it lasts until September 14th.
Clerk	That's right, madam.

Anne	Excuse me. What time does the Manchester train leave?
Guard	Which one? The fast train or the slow one?
Anne	The fast one.
Guard	It leaves at nine o'clock.
Anne	Which platform does it leave from?
Guard	Platform number seven.
Anne	And how long does the journey take?
Guard	It takes about two and a half hours.
Anne	Thank you very much.

Practice

a What's the date today?
   It's May the ninth.

b ....
   ....

c ....
   ....

d ....

e ....

f ....

Train timetable
Mondays — Fridays

Platform	Destination	Departure	Arrival
5	Birmingham	8.30	10.00
7	Manchester	9.00	11.30
3	Chester	9.30	12.00
8	Rugby	10.00	11.00
9	Glasgow	11.00	4.00 (16.00)
6	Liverpool	11.30	2.00 (14.00)

Ask and answer questions about the trains like this:

What time does the Manchester train leave?

It leaves at nine o'clock.

Which platform does it leave from?

Platform number seven.

And how long does the journey take?

It takes about two and a half hours.

Write one of your conversations here:

....
....
....
....
....
....

Where	do	I you we they	come from. live. stay.
	she does	he	

I You We They	come from Italy. stay at the Hilton Hotel. live in Tokyo.
He She	comes from France. stays at the Plaza Hotel. lives in Istanbul.

Do you usually clean windows at midnight?

David Steele	Good evening, Wilson.
Steve Wilson	Oh . . . er . . . good evening, Mr. Steele.
David	What are you doing up there, Wilson?
Steve	I'm . . . er . . . cleaning the windows.
David	Do you usually clean windows at midnight?
Steve	Er . . . no.

David	Who lives here?
Steve	Mrs Hartley.
David	And does Mrs Hartley know you are here?
Steve	Er . . . no. She is away.
David	And where is she?
Steve	I think she's on holiday.

David	Wilson?
Steve	Yes.
David	How often do you clean Mrs Hartley's windows?
Steve	Er . . . about once a month.
David	And how much does she pay you?
Steve	Nothing. I do it free.

David	So you do it free, do you?
Steve	Yes.
David	That's good. I'm looking for a window cleaner.
Steve	But . . . . . .
David	Come along, Wilson. I've got a nice little job for you.
Steve	Where?
David	At the police station. There are sixty eight windows there and I want you to clean them.

Mike Wilson and his family are on holiday in Southend.

This is what they are doing today:

a　　　　　　　　　　b　　　　　　　　　　c　　　　　　　　　　d

This is what they usually do:

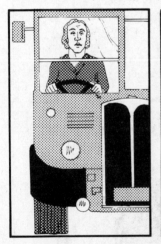   

a　　　　　　　　　　b　　　　　　　　　　c　　　　　　　　　　d

Write sentences like this.

a　　Today Mike Wilson is driving a car. Mike Wilson usually drives a bus.
a　　　　Mike Wilson usually drives a bus but today he is driving a car.
b　　_____
b　　_____
c　　_____
c　　_____
d　　_____
d　　_____

Write more sentences about the Wilson family using these words: eats, watches, wears.

Money doesn't grow on trees

Pat	Mike! Look at the floor!
Mike	What's wrong with it?
Pat	What's wrong with it! It's filthy!
Mike	Oh . . . .
Pat	It's filthy because you never wipe your shoes.
Mike	Sorry, love.

Pat	What are you looking for now?
Mike	My cigarettes.
Pat	Well they're not here. They're in the dustbin.
Mike	In the dustbin! Why?
Pat	Because there's cigarette ash on every carpet in the house.
Mike	I don't drop ash on the carpets.
Pat	Oh yes you do. I know because I hoover them.

Pat	Anyway, cigarettes are a waste of money.
Mike	Maybe they are, but I earn the money! It doesn't grow on trees you know.
Mike	I work 8 hours a day. Remember?
Pat	Well, what about my money then?
Mike	What do you mean 'your money'? You don't go out to work, do you?
Pat	No. I don't go out to work. I work 15 hours a day . . . here!
Mike	Well, housework is different . . .
Pat	Oh, I see . . . so house-work is different, is it? House-work doesn't matter. Well you do it then.
Mike	Hey, wait a minute, Pat. Pat . . . . .

Practice

I You We They	go don't go	out to work.
He She	goes doesn't go	

Money doesn't grow on trees. Do these things grow on trees?

apples tomatoes spaghetti coffee rice potatoes lemons pineapples

The floor is always filthy.
Why?
It's filthy because he never wipes his shoes.
_____
_____

George always looks untidy.
Why?
He looks untidy because _____
_____
_____

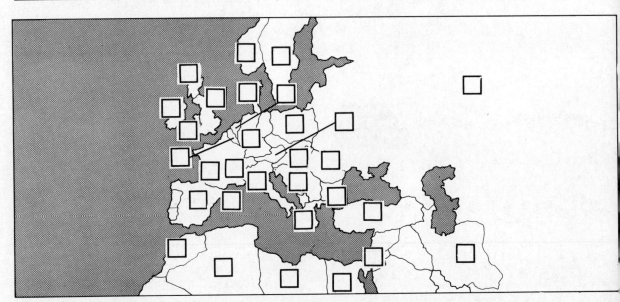

Fill in these countries on the map. Put the numbers in the boxes.

1 Denmark,   2 Holland,   3 France,   4 Greece,   5 Spain,   6 Iran,   7 Egypt,   8 Germany,   9 England,
10 Wales,   11 Sweden,   12 Turkey,   13 Algeria,   14 Portugal,   15 Ireland,   16 Austria,   17 Italy,
18 Russia,   19 Scotland,   20 Norway,   21 Morroco,   22 Lybia,   23 Roumania,   24 Belgium,
25 Yugoslavia,   26 Hungary,   27 Bulgaria,   28 Switzerland,   29 Poland,   30 Jordan.

What languages do they speak in these countries?

It's half past six

Cathy	Come on, darling. We haven't got much time.
Brian	All right. I'm nearly ready. What time does the bus leave?
Cathy	Half past six . . . and it's quarter past six already.
Brian	Oh, we've got plenty of time.
Cathy	We haven't. Hurry up!
Brian	All right. Let's go.
Cathy	And about time too!

Brian	Two to Shaftesbury Avenue, please.
Conductor	That's 50p.
Brian	Do you know what time the last bus leaves Shaftesbury Avenue?
Conductor	Yes, the last 24 leaves at quarter to twelve.
Cathy	Do any other buses go to Hampstead?
Conductor	Yes, the 28 and the 187. I think the last 28 leaves at midnight.
Cathy	And the 187?
Conductor	I'm afraid I don't know. You can check at the bus stop.
Brian	O.K. Thanks.

Practice

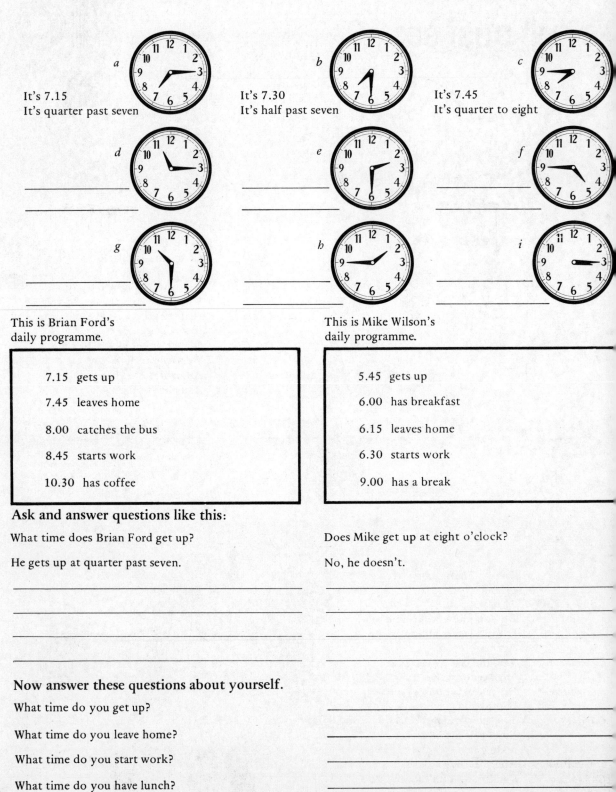

a It's 7.15 It's quarter past seven
b It's 7.30 It's half past seven
c It's 7.45 It's quarter to eight

d _____
e _____
f _____

g _____
h _____
i _____

This is Brian Ford's daily programme.

7.15	gets up
7.45	leaves home
8.00	catches the bus
8.45	starts work
10.30	has coffee

This is Mike Wilson's daily programme.

5.45	gets up
6.00	has breakfast
6.15	leaves home
6.30	starts work
9.00	has a break

Ask and answer questions like this:

What time does Brian Ford get up?

He gets up at quarter past seven.

_____
_____
_____
_____

Does Mike get up at eight o'clock?

No, he doesn't.

_____
_____
_____
_____

Now answer these questions about yourself.

What time do you get up? _____

What time do you leave home? _____

What time do you start work? _____

What time do you have lunch? _____

What time do you go to bed? _____

Don't stay out late

Steve	I'm going out Mum.
Mrs Wilson	Where are you going?
Steve	To the disco.

Mrs Wilson	All right, but don't stay out all night.
Steve	O.K.
Mrs Wilson	And don't spend all your money.
Steve	All right.

Mrs Wilson	And don't get into trouble.
Steve	Mum?
Mrs Wilson	Yes?
Steve	Don't worry about me. Bye.

What are these people saying?

cross　　　　　　　　　　　　　　　　a

smoke　　　　　　　　　　　　　　　b

walk　　　　　　　　　　　　　　　　c

park　　　　　　　　　　　　　　　　d

Practice

Mike Wilson is a bus driver and he earns £80 a week.

He lives in a small house in East London with his wife and his two children.

Mike works from half past six in the morning until four o'clock in the afternoon. In the evenings he usually watches television.

On Saturday evenings Mike always goes to the pub with his friends but on Sundays he usually washes his car or visits his mother.

Question

1 What is Mike's job?

2 Does he live in Manchester?

3 Where does he live?

4 Is he married?

5 How many children has he got?

6 What time does Mike start work?

7 How many hours a day does he work?

8 How much money does he earn?

9 What does he do in the evenings?

10 Does he go to the cinema on Saturdays?

11 Who does he go to the pub with?

12 What does he do on Sundays?

Now write about Brian Ford.

Brian Ford/businessman/£650 a month. He/flat/ North London/wife/three children. Brian/8.45/ 6 o'clock. evenings/newspaper. Saturday/plays golf/ Sundays/for a walk/his friends.

Can you play the guitar?

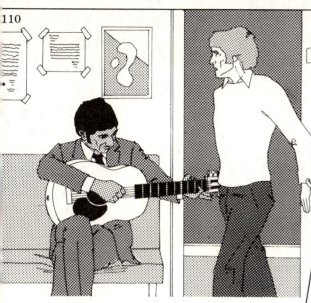

Chris	What an awful noise!
Gordon	What do you mean? Can you play the guitar?
Chris	Yes, I can.
Gordon	All right. Here you are.

Gordon	That sounds terrible. You can't play the guitar!
Chris	Of course it sounds terrible. I'm tuning it.
Gordon	Oh, sorry.

Gordon	That's nice. Can you read music?
Chris	Yes.
Gordon	Can you play this?

Chris	Er . . . I think so. Can you hold it for me?
Gordon	O.K.
Chris	I can't read it. Can you hold it the right way up?

Practice

a

Chris _____
Gordon _____

c

Gordon _____
Chris _____

b

Chris _____
Gordon _____

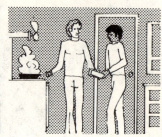
d

Gordon _____
Chris _____

e

Look at this:

Can he play golf?

Yes, he can.

Now you do the same with these pictures.

f

g

h

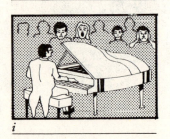
i

j

k

Answer these questions.

Can you play the guitar? Can you drive? Can you swim? Can you type? Can you speak Russian? Can you read Chinese?

A rule is a rule

Chris	Hello Peter.
Peter	I'm sorry, you can't come in here.
Gordon	What? Why not?
Peter	Because you're wearing jeans.
Chris	But . . . Peter you know us.
Peter	I'm sorry, you can't come in. We've got a new manager.
Gordon	This is silly.
Peter	Look, I can't let you in.
Manager	What's the trouble Peter?
Peter	Nothing Mr Phillips . . . . Well, they're wearing jeans . . . . . . but they're old friends. Can they come in?
Manager	No, they can't. A rule is a rule.
Gordon	So we can't come in!
Manager	No, I'm sorry you can't All the other customers are wearing suits and ties.
Gordon	Come on Chris. Let's go somewhere else.

Practice

| Can | you
he
she

we
you
they | paint?
dance?
cook?
type?
run?
sing?
drive? |

| Yes,

No, | I
you
he
she
it
we
you
they | can.

can't. |

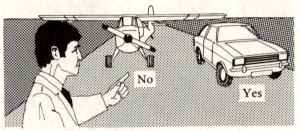

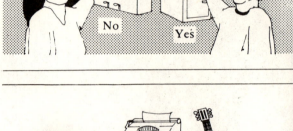

You write: He can drive a car but he can't fly an aeroplane.

Look at these.

1 go in/smoking ... He can't go in because he's smoking.
2 watch TV/got one ... He can't watch television because he hasn't got one.

Now you make some sentences.

    1 answer phone/bath   7 read newspaper/wearing glasses
    2 drive/got licence   8 go theatre/got tickets
    3 listen radio/eating   9 play garden/raining
    4 play football/wearing boots   10 understand student/speaking French
    5 look visual/got book   11 go restaurant/wearing jeans
    6 write exercise/got pen

Now ask the person next to you why he or she can't do these things.

    Why can't you drive a car?
    Because I haven't got a licence.

I'm going to take an X-ray

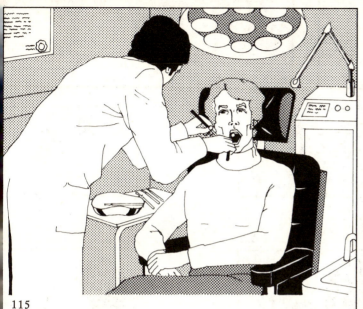

115

Dentist	Now, open your mouth, please.
Chris	Ummmmmm.
Dentist	Open wide, please.
Chris	Ahh!
Dentist	Thank you.

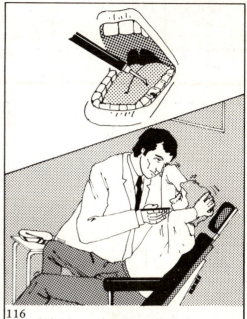

116

Chris	Is it going to hurt?
Dentist	No, it isn't.
Chris	Ow!
Dentist	Well, not very much.

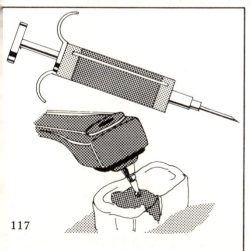

117

Chris	Are you going to give me an injection?
Dentist	Not at the moment.
Chris	Well, are you going to do any fillings?
Dentist	Not yet . . .

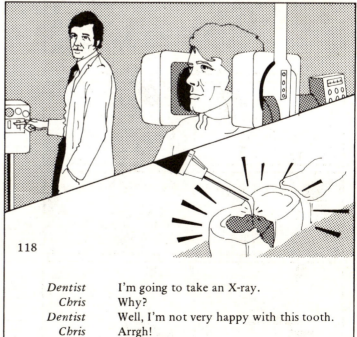

118

Dentist	I'm going to take an X-ray.
Chris	Why?
Dentist	Well, I'm not very happy with this tooth.
Chris	Arrgh!

Practice

I'm you're he's she's	going to	have an injection. see the dentist. do some fillings. take an X-ray.
It's	going to	hurt. rain.

Am I Are you Is he Is she	going to	have an injection. see the dentist. do some fillings. take an X-ray.	?
Is it	going to	hurt. rain.	?

a

You write
Is she going to
wash her hair?

b

c

d

e

f

g

You write: He's going to get up and then he's going to have breakfast.

h

i

j

What are they going to do?

Anne Why is that bulldozer there?
Chris They're going to knock down the pub
Anne Oh no! That's a beautiful old pub!
Chris I know, it's a shame, isn't it?

Anne A shame! It's a scandal. What are they going to build there?
Chris Oh, a new supermarket.
Anne But we don't need a new supermarket.
We've got three already.

Chris Then they're going to knock down the Post Office next door and build some offices there.
Anne Right! That's enough!

Chris What are you going to do?
Anne I'm going to stop them.

Practice

What are you		do?
What's he	going to	buy?
What are they		build?

We're		knock it down.
They're	going to	build a new house.

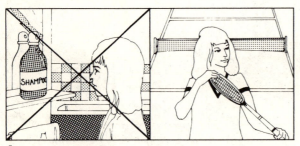

a

You write Is she going to wash her hair? No, she isn't. She's going to play tennis.

b

c

d

e

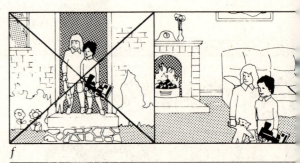

f

Ask the student sitting next to you "going to" questions.

Which programme/television tonight?
Which shoes/tomorrow?
What/for dinner tomorrow?
Which teacher/this afternoon?

What time/up tomorrow?
Which bus/home this evening?
What/tomorrow?
What/this weekend?

Revision

Ask and answer questions like this:

Prompt	passport
You ask:	Has he got a passport?
	Yes, he has.
	Where is it?
	It's in his pocket.

Prompt	wine
You ask:	Has she got any wine?
	No, she hasn't.

Prompts	passport	cigarettes
	wine	newspaper
	watch	hat
	keys	books
	rings	lighter

Prompts	wine	milk
	eggs	tomatoes
	pen	cat
	dog	apples
	butter	basket

Mrs Wilson	Where are you going, Kevin?
Kevin	Out.
Pat	Out where?
Kevin	Out to the garden.
Pat	Please put on your coat.
Kevin	Why?
Pat	Because it's cold.
Kevin	It isn't cold.
Pat	Kevin?
Kevin	Yes.
Pat	Put on your coat.
Kevin	Oh all right, but it isn't cold.

Pat Wilson	Where/Mike? _____
Mike	_____
Pat	_____
Mike	pub. _____
Pat	take/umbrella. _____
Mike	_____
Pat	raining. _____
Mike	_____
Pat	_____
Mike	_____
Pat	take/umbrella. _____
Mike	

a

Information

Surname: Wilson
First names: Michael Henry
Profession: Bus Driver
Single/Married: Married
Children: Two
Height: Five foot eleven inches (1m 80)
Colour of eyes: Blue
Colour of hair: Brown

b

Information

Surname: Goodwin
First Names: Sarah Jane
Profession: Reporter
Single/Married: Single
Children: —
Height: Five foot six inches (1m 68)
Colour of eyes: Green
Colour of hair: Fair

Michael Wilson is a bus driver.
He's got blue eyes and brown hair.
He's five feet eleven inches tall.
He's married and he's got two children.

Describe Sarah Goodwin.

_____
_____
_____
_____

Complete these forms.

Another person — c

Information

Surname:
First names:
Profession:
Single/Married:
Children:
Height:
Colour of eyes:
Colour of hair:

You — d

Information

Surname:
First names:
Profession:
Single/Married:
Children:
Height:
Colour of eyes:
Colour of hair:

Now write the descriptions.

_____
_____
_____
_____

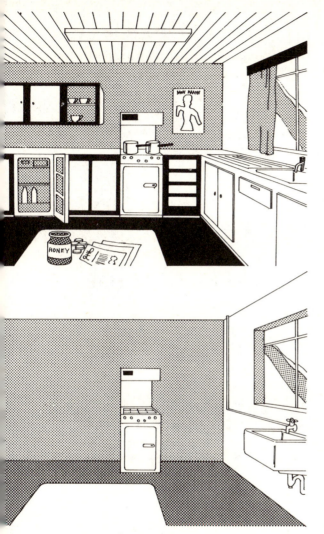

Ask and answer questions about this picture.

1. How/pictures/wall?
   There/pictures/wall.
2. How/money/table?
   There/pounds/table.
3. How/saucepans/cooker?
   There/saucepan/cooker.
4. How/cups/cupboard?
   There/cups/cupboard.
5. How/milk/fridge?
   There/bottles/fridge.
6. How/honey/jar?
   There/half a kilo/jar.

**Look at both kitchens.
What is missing in this kitchen?**

_____
_____
_____
_____
_____
_____
_____
_____

What are these people saying?

Morning trains				Evening trains			
Guildford	7.30	8.00	8.15	Waterloo	17.15	17.30	17.45
Woking	7.45	8.15	8.30	Surbiton		17.45	18.00
Weybridge	8.00			Weybridge		18.00	
Surbiton	8.15		9.00	Woking	17.45	18.15	18.30
Waterloo	8.30	8.45	9.15	Guildford	18.00	18.30	18.45

Answer these questions about the morning train:

1. What time does the seven-thirty train arrive at Waterloo? _____
2. Where does the eight o'clock train stop? _____
3. Does the eight-fifteen train stop at Weybridge? _____
4. Does the eight-fifteen train stop at Woking? _____
5. What time does the eight-fifteen train arrive at Surbiton? _____
6. How many times does the seven-thirty train stop? _____

Now make questions about the evening train:

1. _____ It arrives at six o'clock. (1800).
2. _____ It stops at Surbiton and Woking.
3. _____ No, it doesn't.
4. _____ Yes, it does.
5. _____ At six forty five. (1845).
6. _____ It stops twice.

Every morning Anne Scott leaves her house at seven-thirty and walks to Guildford station. She usually catches the eight o'clock train to London but sometimes she catches the eight-fifteen train. On the way the train stops at Woking and a lot of passengers get on there. The train arrives at Waterloo station at eight-forty-five. Anne gets to her office at nine o'clock.

Write about Anne Scott's evening journey from her office to her home.

Write about your journey from your home to work or to school.

Revision

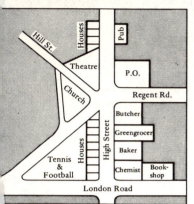

Now. → In the next ten years.

Use the following words to describe what's going to happen to the town:
knock down, build, widen, make, leave, close.

Butchers _____   Car park _____
Pub _____   High Street _____
Roundabout _____   Hill Street _____

What else are they going to do? Write six more sentences.

What's he doing?
What's he going to do next?

What's he doing now?
What's he going to do next?

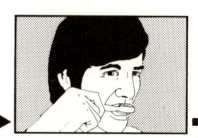

What's he doing now?
What's he going to do next?

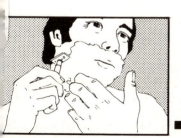

Is he going to have a bath next?
What's he going to do?

Is he going to feed the cat next?
What's he going to do?

Is he going to watch TV next?
What's he going to do next?

Write down the next six things you think he's going to do.

Write down what you are going to do today.

THE GOLDEN LION HOTEL
The Golden Lion Hotel, Medway Avenue, Clifton, Bristol 5

May 3rd, 1977.

Dear Cathy,

How are you and Brian? We are all fine. At the moment we are staying in a hotel because our new house isn't ready yet. The workmen are still painting the outside. The house is very attractive and it's got a small garden and a garage. There are four bedrooms so when are you going to come and stay with us?

Bristol is a very pleasant city. It's got a large modern shopping centre and lots of parks. There are a few old buildings like the cathedral and the university, and there is a very famous theatre called 'The Bristol Old Vic'. John says he is going to take me to the theatre for my birthday next month. I hope he dosen't forget!

John likes his new job but it's very hard work. He leaves the hotel at 7.30 every morning and he doesn't get back until after 8.00 p.m. Next week he's going to get a company car so on Saturday we are going to visit my sister in Weston-super-mare.

We miss London and all our friends but we like Bristol a lot.

Please write soon and tell us all your news.

With love from
Elizabeth

Answer these questions
1. Where does Cathy live?
2. Where do John and Elizabeth live?
3. Why are John and Elizabeth staying in a hotel?
4. What is the name of the hotel?
5. Has their new house got a garage?
6. How many bedrooms are there?
7. Is there a university at Bristol?
8. What is the name of the theatre?
9. Why is John going to take Elizabeth to the theatre next month?
10. What time does John leave the hotel in the mornings?
11. Does he like his job?
12. What is he going to get next week?
13. Where are they going to drive on Saturday?
14. Whose sister lives in Weston-super-Mare?
15. Do John and Elizabeth like Bristol?

Make questions for these answers
1. There are four bedrooms.
2. Next March.
3. After 8.00 p.m.
4. Elizabeth's sister.
5. No, they are painting the outside of the house

Correct these statements
1. They are staying in a pub in Bath.
2. The house is very unattractive. It's got a large garden and a shed.
3. Bristol has got an old shopping centre and a few parks.
4. Elizabeth's birthday is in July and John is going to take her to the cinema.
5. John doesn't like his new job and he hates living in Bristol.